THE THREE Rs

REDUCE, REUSE, AND RECYCLE

E-WASTE

Candice Letkeman

LIGHTBOX
openlightbox.com

LIGHTBOX

Go to
www.openlightbox.com
and enter this book's
unique code.

ACCESS CODE

LBXB7265

Lightbox is an all-inclusive digital solution for the teaching and learning of curriculum topics in an original, groundbreaking way. Lightbox is based on National Curriculum Standards.

OPTIMIZED FOR

- ✓ TABLETS
- ✓ WHITEBOARDS
- ✓ COMPUTERS
- ✓ AND MUCH MORE!

STANDARD FEATURES OF LIGHTBOX

AUDIO High-quality narration using text-to-speech system

VIDEOS Embedded high-definition video clips

ACTIVITIES Printable PDFs that can be emailed and graded

WEBLINKS Curated links to external, child-safe resources

SLIDESHOWS Pictorial overviews of key concepts

INTERACTIVE MAPS Interactive maps and aerial satellite imagery

QUIZZES Ten multiple choice questions that are automatically graded and emailed for teacher assessment

KEY WORDS Matching key concepts to their definitions

VIDEOS

WEBLINKS

SLIDESHOWS

QUIZZES

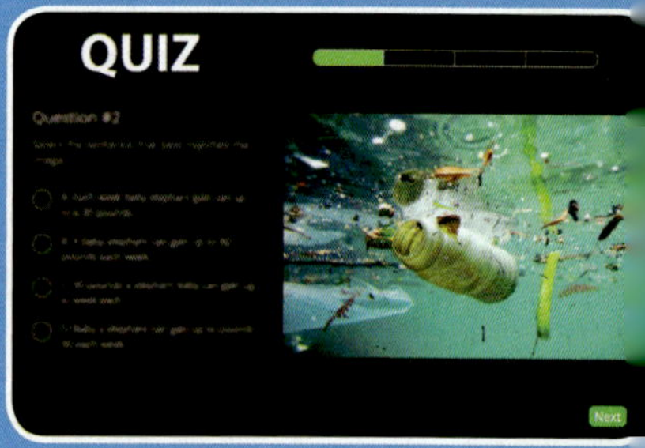

In this book, you will learn

what e-waste is,

how it affects Earth,

how you can help,

and much more!

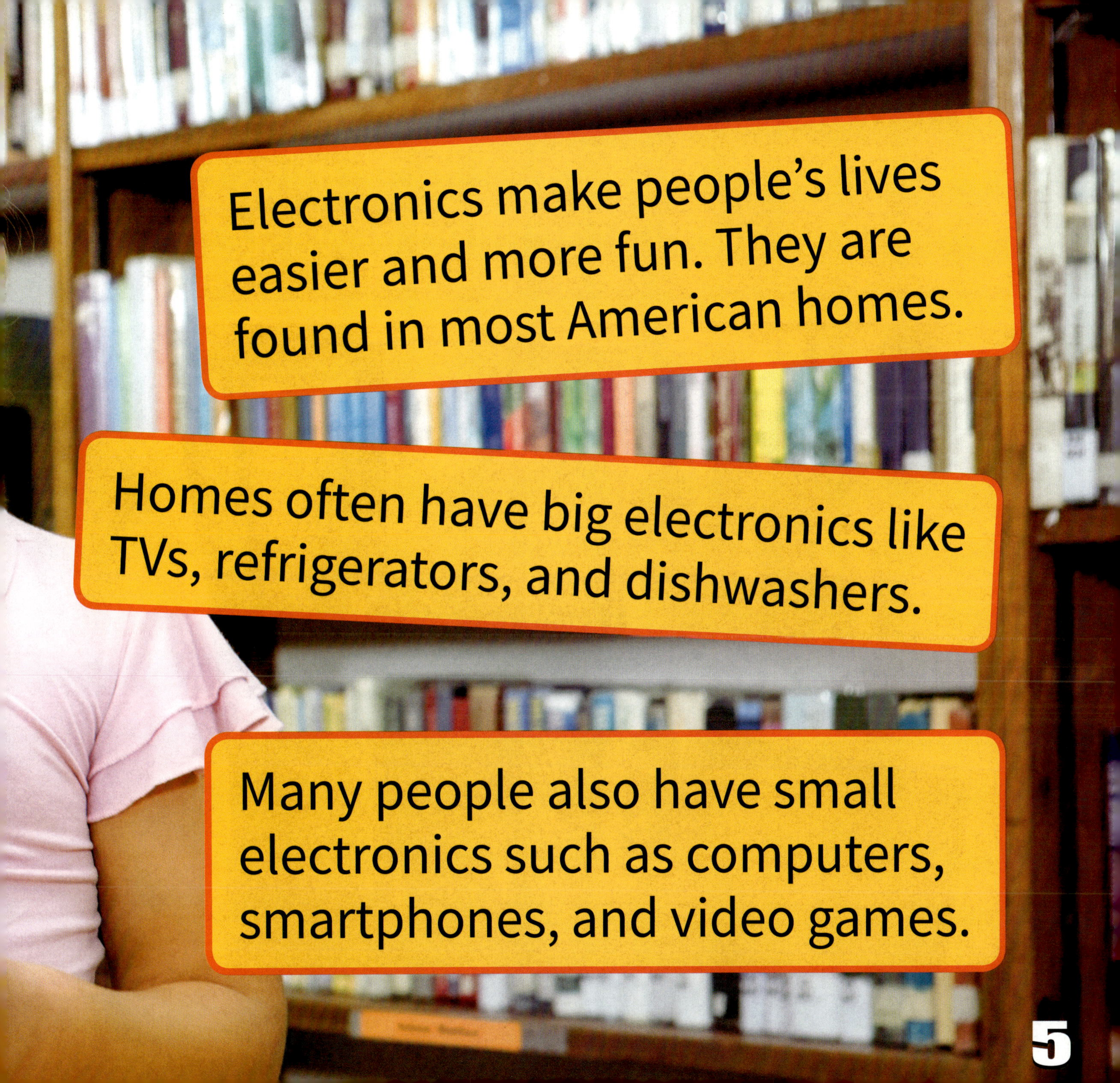

Electronics make people's lives easier and more fun. They are found in most American homes.

Homes often have big electronics like TVs, refrigerators, and dishwashers.

Many people also have small electronics such as computers, smartphones, and video games.

When electronics get old or broken we throw them away. Electronics that we throw away are called e-waste.

Computers and cell phones that are no longer being used are e-waste. Most e-waste ends up in landfills.

About **350,000 cell phones** are **thrown out** in the United States **every day**.

The inside of some electronics can harm people and Earth. E-waste in landfills can poison the air and water.

Most e-waste from the United States is sent to other countries such as China.

Guiyu, **China**, was once called the **e-waste capital** of the **world**.

We need to work together to keep e-waste out of landfills.

The **Three Rs** is an easy plan that helps us do just that. It has three steps.

These are **reduce**, **reuse**, and **recycle**.

Reduce how much e-waste you make.
Reduce means to make less.

Broken electronics can often be fixed instead of being thrown away.
This keeps e-waste out of landfills.

Use your electronics longer before buying new ones. This reduces the number of new electronics you need to buy.

There are many ways to **reuse** old electronics.

You can use an old smartphone just as a camera. You could also use it just to play music.

You could reuse an old laptop to watch movies. An old webcam can be used to see who is at your door.

You can give your old electronics to someone who needs them. A charity can find new homes for old devices.

Some electronics stores buy old devices and fix them. These used devices are then sold at lower prices.

You can help keep e-waste out of landfills by **recycling** it.

Recycling **1 million** laptops **saves** the amount **of energy** used by **3,657** American homes in **one year**.

Parts from old electronics can be made into new ones. Some electronics have gold, silver, or platinum in them.

How can you follow the **Three Rs**?
Think about your home, your school,
and your neighborhood.

Reduce

How can you reduce the e-waste
your family makes?

Reuse

Who could reuse electronics
that you no longer want?

Recycle

What can you do to make sure e-waste
gets recycled at your school?

E-WASTE FACTS

These pages provide detailed information that expands on the interesting facts found in the book. They are intended to be used by adults as a learning support to help young readers round out their knowledge of reducing, reusing, or recycling each kind of object or material featured in *The Three Rs* series.

Pages 4–5

The average American home has 24 electronic products. These include large and small appliances, as well as personal electronic devices such as computers, printers, and cell phones. Radios, TVs, electric tools, such as drills and saws, toys, and video games are all different kinds of electronics. When these appliances or devices break down and are thrown away, they are considered e-waste.

Pages 6–7

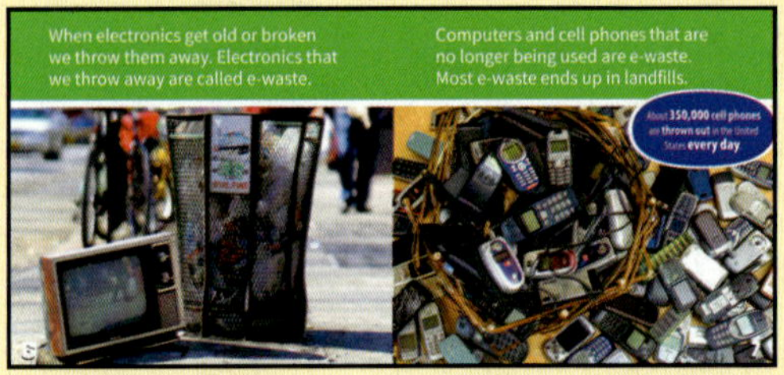

E-waste is the term used to describe discarded electronics and electrical products. More than 127 million cell phones are thrown away annually in the United States. Since technology changes very quickly, most electronics are replaced after only a few years. Although nearly 100 percent of e-waste is recyclable, most of the e-waste produced globally is not. The Environmental Protection Agency (EPA) estimates that 50 billion tons (45 metric tons) of e-waste enters landfills each year.

Pages 8–9

The e-waste capital of the world is Guiyu, China. Nearly 70 percent of the world's e-waste ends up in China. People in Guiyu burn the plastics and pour acids on the circuit boards to recover their steel and copper. This puts harmful pollutants, including lead and mercury, into the air and water. Children of parents who take apart circuit-boards for work are most affected by exposure to lead. High levels of lead in young children can impact the development of their central nervous system and intelligence.

Pages 10–11

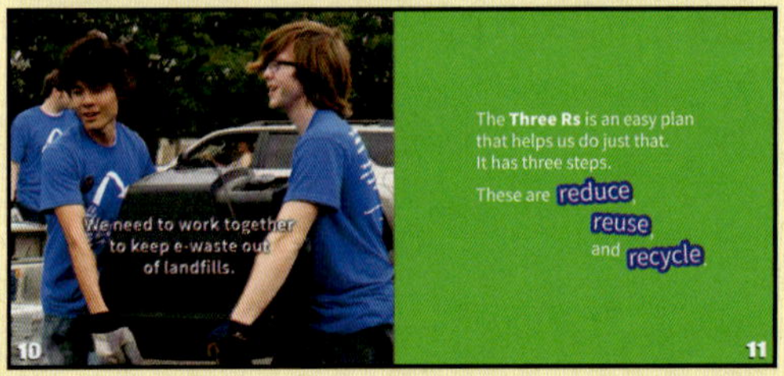

What can be done with old electronics? Reduce, reuse, and recycle applies to e-waste just as much as it does to any other type of recyclable materials. You can reduce e-waste by buying devices that have been refurbished or produced in an environmentally safe way. You can also maintain the electronics you own. Donating electronics that still work so they can be reused helps keep them out of the landfill. Recycling is the best plan for items that cannot be reused.

Pages 12–13

Refurbished electronics have been renewed in some way. Sometimes, a cracked screen or other broken piece has been replaced. Often, refurbished devices are just fine, but must be labeled as refurbished because the packaging was once opened or damaged. Consumers may be nervous about buying refurbished products because they perceive these items as inferior to new ones. However, most refurbished electronics are as good as new and often come with the same warranty and tech support.

Pages 14–15

Some electronic devices are easier to fix than you might think. It can be fun and satisfying to take things apart and make them work again. Video game consoles or personal music players are good projects to start with. There are many free video guides online that will step you through common repairs. Learning how to take things apart and put them back together properly is a very valuable skill. Consider starting a gadget repair club, or make a project of taking something apart and fixing it.

Pages 16–17

What if all devices had a second life? Some companies collect, refurbish, and redistribute used cell phones. Many computer companies have take-back programs that allow people to return old computers or phones when they no longer need them. These computers are refurbished and resold at considerable discounts. Other companies will accept and recycle all kinds of used electronics, no matter where they were bought or how old they are.

Pages 18–19

Only 12.5 percent of e-waste is currently recycled in the United States. For every 1 million phones that are recycled, about 17.6 tons (16 metric tons) of copper, 770 pounds (350 kg) of silver, and 75 pounds (34 kg) of gold are recovered. However, many e-waste recycling businesses ship the waste to developing countries, where the recycling practices are harmful to the people and the planet.

Pages 20–21

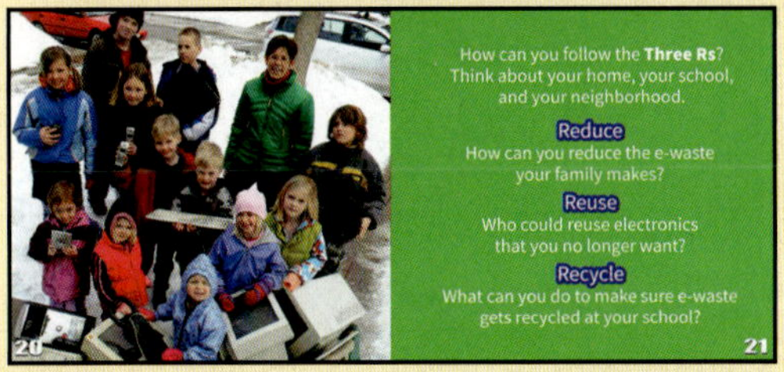

Recycling e-waste helps recover natural resources. Salvaging silver and gold from electronics is better for the environment than mining for them. E-waste recyclers who practice on-site recycling are fairly common in Europe, but less so in the United States. Workers at e-waste recycling facilities wear protective gear and manually take the pieces apart and sort them. Machines further break the pieces down to the point where they can be reused. Which of the Three Rs is the most important in managing e-waste?

KEY WORDS

Research has shown that as much as 65 percent of all written material published in English is made up of 300 words. These 300 words cannot be taught using pictures or learned by sounding them out. They must be recognized by sight. This book contains 101 common sight words to help young readers improve their reading fluency and comprehension. This book also teaches young readers several important content words, such as proper nouns. These words are paired with pictures to aid in learning and improve understanding.

Page	Sight Words First Appearance
5	also, American, and, are, as, big, found, have, homes, in, like, lives, make, many, more, most, often, people, small, such, they
6	away, get, old, or, that, them, we, when
7	about, being, day, ends, every, no, out, states, up
8	air, can, Earth, of, some, the, water
9	from, is, once, other, to, was, world
10	keep, need, together, work
11	an, do, has, helps, it, just, these, three, us
12	be, how, means, much, this, you
13	before, new, number, ones, use, your
14	a, could, play, there, ways
15	at, see, watch, who
16	find, for, give
17	then
18	by, year
19	each, into, made, parts
21	family, school, think, want, what

Page	Content Words First Appearance
5	computers, dishwashers, electronics, refrigerators, smartphones, TVs, video games
6	e-waste
7	cell phones, landfills, United States
9	China, countries, e-waste capital, Guiyu
11	plan, recycle, reduce, reuse, steps, Three Rs
14	camera, music
15	door, laptop, movies, webcam
16	charity, devices
17	prices, stores
18	energy
19	gold, platinum, silver
21	neighborhood

Published by Smartbook Media Inc.
350 5th Avenue, 59th Floor New York, NY 10118
Website: www.openlightbox.com

Library of Congress Control Number: 2018941517

ISBN 978-1-5105-4001-9 (hardcover)
ISBN 978-1-5105-4002-6 (multi-user eBook)

062018
120117

Printed in Brainerd, Minnesota, United States
1 2 3 4 5 6 7 8 9 0 22 21 20 19 18

Project Coordinator: Jared Siemens
Designer: Terry Paulhus

Every reasonable effort has been made to trace ownership and to obtain permission to reprint copyright material. The publisher would be pleased to have any errors or omissions brought to its attention so that they may be corrected in subsequent printings.

The publisher acknowledges Alamy, Getty Images, iStock, Shutterstock, Newscom, and Dreamstime as its primary image suppliers for this title.